This book belongs to
a girl with an incredible heart
and a sparkling soul: you!

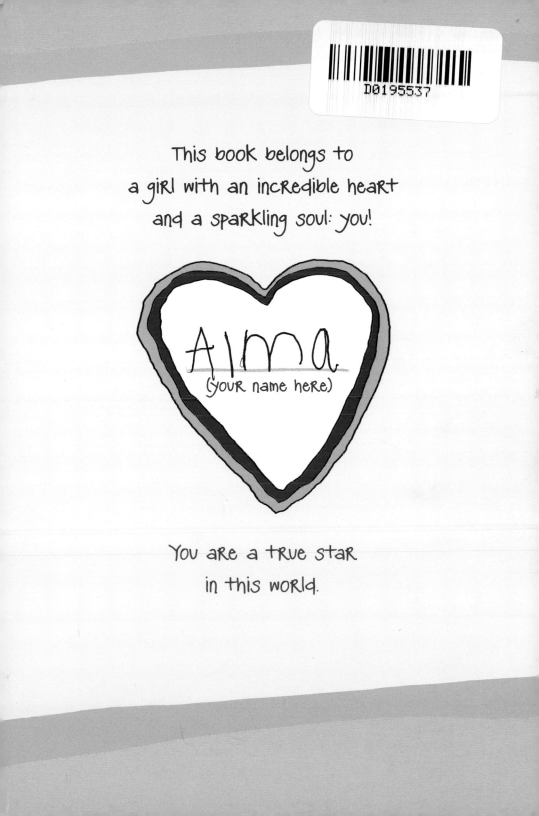

Alma

(your name here)

You are a true star
in this world.

Titles by Ashley Rice
Published by
Blue Mountain Arts®

For an Incredible Kid
Girl Power
Girls Rule
Sisters Are Forever Friends
You Are a Girl Who Totally Rocks!
You Go, Girl... Keep Dreaming

For an Incredible Girl/Para una niña increíble
(Bilingual Edition)

Library of Congress Control Number: 2009903447
ISBN: 978-1-59842-351-8

BLUE MOUNTAIN PRESS is registered in U.S. Patent and Trademark Office.

Certain trademarks are used under license.

Printed in China.
Fifth Printing: 2012

Blue Mountain Arts, Inc.
P.O. Box 4549, Boulder, Colorado 80306

You Are a Girl Who Totally Rocks!

Always Be True
to You!

Ashley Rice

Blue Mountain Press™

Boulder, Colorado

Introduction

Being a girl who rocks means a lot of things. It means being happy with the person you are and the person you are becoming. It means celebrating all the little things that make you unique — like your freckles or your special talents or your sense of humor. It means following your heart and singing your own song.

Mostly, being a girl who rocks is about being true to yourself — always — because when you are true to yourself, you have the courage to express who you are with originality and enthusiasm. You aren't afraid to step out from the crowd and take chances and make a difference in the world.

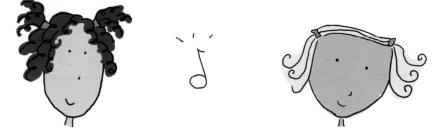

Of course, being true to yourself isn't always easy; there are so many different ideas about who and how and what to be. And there's a lot of pressure out there to be someone you're not. That's where this book comes in. It's full of powerful words to inspire you to face each day with confidence and stay true to yourself no matter what.

So whether you're having one of those days where you're feeling great and everything is going your way or one of those days where you're feeling a little unsure of yourself, this book has just the right words for you. It will help you remember that you are a shining star in this world and that you can do anything because... you are a girl who totally rocks.

Be * True * to You!

*B*eing true to yourself takes guts. First, you've got to face everything around you and figure out what is important: what you think really counts. Second, you've got to interact with a lot of people who may see things differently. But life has lots of smiles and frowns, as days have their own ups and downs. And if you are true to yourself in all that you do, and if you keep working to make your dreams come true... then you will achieve success just by doing your best.

You've got everything it takes to be true to you.

The Absolutely True Story of One Amazing Girl... You!

Once there was a girl and she was unique and talented and interesting and amazing and unforgettable... and real. She knew, deep down, that if she tried something and it didn't go as she had hoped or wanted or dreamed or planned, she could just try something different — or try the same thing again but approach it in a new or different way — and one day her greatest hopes and dreams could actually come true...

And so her life was full of amazing and unforgettable moments, events, and circumstances: incredible wins, of course, but also equally incredible — and worth it — losses. No matter what happened, she learned from everything around her and everything she went through. Yes, she fell sometimes (like everybody else does), but she got up and moved forward by always being true to herself. And maybe one day she will even make a path for others to follow... until they can make their own paths, too.

You see, it's not that she was never frightened or sad or even knew when she woke up each day what to do (no one does). It was simply that she believed in herself and always shined on like a star. Just like you.

Believe

Believe in the person you **are** and the person you are **becoming**. Don't let hurt feelings or misunderstandings stop you from **reaching out** for your great **dreams**. Love each day and **cherish** the moments that make up your days. Change the world for the **better**.

Be Bold

Live and make **friends** boldly.
Believe in your hopes,
dreams, skills, and **stars**.
Have **patience** and never, ever
waver from **hope**.
Be who you are.
You are an **incredible** girl.

Girls Who Rock Are Discoverers of New Paths

They are trailblazers and
superheroines and confidantes.
They make their way with courage,
strength, humor, and love.
They know how to laugh and to listen,
to dare and to try.
They don't give up when
the going gets tough.

They are students and seekers,
learners and keepers
of goals and dreams
and of the unexpected.
They believe in themselves
and reach for the stars.

You Are a Girl Who Rocks

YOU:

The **words** you say...

the **friends** you make...

the **stuff** you know...

the **RISKS** you take...

the way you **deal** with things...

and the life you make every day...

(These
aRe all
paRts of what
make you so
gReat.)

You Have the Power

The power to be oneself is perhaps one of the best gifts a person can both "have" and – at the same time – "give." It is when we are our true selves that we find our best friends, write our best lines, and score the most points on the never-ending tests that are placed before us. It is when we are our true selves that we discover things we have in common with others who are on similar paths and are being themselves and following their hearts, too. It is when we are ourselves that we shine the brightest, laugh the loudest, and learn the most.

Being ourselves often includes times we have
to Run ahead OR wait behind... It's when we
aRe ourselves that we can pass on couRage to
another person. This is the "gift" part and
the Reason why being oneself is never a selfish
act, but one that is Rooted - always, always -
in love, friendship, and couRage.

What Makes You Unique?

You are special.
It's true...
There is no one else quite like you.
So don't hesitate
to step out from the crowd,
to show your own style, your own smile,
your own way of doing things...

Individuality is
one of the greatest
gifts in life.

You Don't Need "Things" to Be Great

You don't have to have the perfect **clothes** or the newest **haircut** or the latest music. You don't have to know the right thing to say all the time. Just be **yourself** and believe in your most amazing hopes and dreams. **Strive** for **excellence**, and don't get frustrated if you make mistakes. Make good **friends**, and be true to **yourself** — that's what's important.

You don't need a long list of **accomplishments** to be great — you already are.

Your Life Rules!

Find pleasure in what lies in
   front of you,
in what you've "got."
What you've got is a lot,
and you've got it for a reason.
Your life will not be exactly like
   any of your friends' lives,
but there is a reason for that,
which begins and ends
with the fact that
   you're <u>YOU</u>.

You've got your own truth,
your own knowledge to uncover,
your own discoveries to make,
your own stories to tell.
Do what you can, and do it well.
Live in the moment, and above all else...

...always be yourself.

Things You Should Know

1. It's impossible to be perfect all the time, and it's okay to make mistakes — they're part of what helps you learn, and they make you who you are.

2. In part, at least, you make your own luck: the more doors you try, the more doors or opportunities will open for you and the more chances will come your way.

And...

3. (Most importantly)...
   You're doing an
   awesome job!

It's not about **how well**
you do...
it's about how hard
you try and what kind
of **person** you are.
There are many
things you'll go through;
there are many
things you will triumph over.
And there will be times
when you'll fall down.

But there will be **MORE**
times when you pull through.
And you will find
greatness in your life.
And you will keep getting
stronger every second
of it.

Some days

you just gotta forget
it all...

...and dance!

Listen...

Sometimes in life there may seem to be no obvious "drummer" — no beat to keep, no path you can see that might set you free or show you the way... or any visible, well-meaning shoulder to lean on for guidance. Well, when that happens...

...listen to yourself. The "drummer" —
the path, the way to get to your
dreams, the "answer" to all of these
things — can be found in your heart.

Just listen.

Sing Your Own Song

Wherever you are
is the place you're in.
It's the way things are.
It's where you're standing right now —
you're learning to follow
your own bright star.
And even if things seem
a little strange to you now,
you'll work your way
through it all, somehow.

Just take a little step,
Reach out further,
get a little closer to
the place where you belong.
In your own skin,
in your own way...
you're singing your own song.

Don't Compare Yourself to Others

Each **PERSON** in the world is special,
   unique, and **iRReplaceable.**
We could not do without any one of them
because then the **STARS** would not
   shine so **bright.**
We would not **leaRn** oR know so much —
noR would ouR smiles let out so much
   bRight **couRage,** hope, and **light.**

You are a **shining** light

in this **world**.

Individuality Rules!

There is greatness in you —
in all that you do,
all that you say,
and in the way you
are a million times
every day.

Be happy.

Be bold.

Be intelligent.

Be energetic.

Be understanding.

Be colorful.

Be creative...

In other words:

just be you!

You're on your way
to amazing
days and dreams.

You've got
the kind of
smile that

stops people
in the street.

And you've got
the kind of
heart with wings...
that will never
let you down.

You totally
ROCK,
sparkle,
shine like
a star,
make a difference
wherever you are.

You Are a Butterfly Girl

You can "fly"
in your own way...
by putting your heart,
your hard work,
and your laugh
into everything you do.

You are someone who can
change the world,
because you always
try your hardest
and do your best.

You are an incredible butterfly girl.

You Will Play Many Roles in Your Life...

Girl, daughter, sister, friend, peer, artist, teammate, student... And in each role you play... leader, actress, neighbor, participant...

...may you find your own way...
star, explorer, expert,
apprentice...

...always striving for fun
and excellence.

You Rock!

Although it's important to **live** in the moment, always **believe** in — and keep working on — tomorrow. And don't underestimate yourself. Acting the part is a lot of becoming the part. If you act **confident**, you are — or **become** — confident. And confidence is one of the most important parts of being successful.

Stay true; **speak** up.
Stand up; stand tall.
Keep **growing**.
Laugh a lot.
Don't worry too much.
Try your hardest.
Dream big...

Stay true to you!

Grow each day
a little more,
knowing what
you're fighting for is
worth something.
Throw yourself into what
you do.
Give your heart
and all you've got.
Have some fun...
work a lot.

You have it in you to
do great things.
You have it in you to
make a difference.
You have it in you to...

live a wonderful life.

Follow Your Heart ♥♥♥

If you are not sure
which way to go...
Ask your heart –
your heart will know.
When your mind
does not know what to say...
Your heart will
find a way.

When you can't see
the finish line
or when your dreams
seem hard to find...

Know that you
know the way:
your heart will
lead you there
one day.

You've got **wisdom** in your soul about the **things** that you love most.

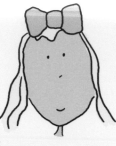

You've got a sense of **humor** that will see you **through** rough days.

You've got a **way** of doing things that is **unique** and all your own.

Hold on to all you've got.

It Takes Guts

It takes guts to dream big dreams.
It takes guts to be who you are.
It takes guts to see big things:
to learn, to grow, and —
knowing what you know —
to move forward in the direction
of your dreams.
It takes guts to dream
these dreams.
It takes guts to stay who you are.

"Guts," of course, is just
another name for courage.
And without it,
we would never
reach the stars.

Girl, you've got guts.

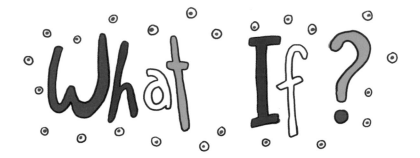

What If?

What would have happened if Amelia Earhart had never gotten on a plane? What if Rosa Parks had decided not to make a stand on that bus? What if Harriet Tubman had been too scared to pioneer the Underground Railroad or if your favorite female novelist had decided writing was too risky or too hard?

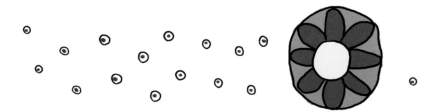

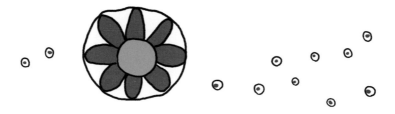

What if all these amazing women had decided not to step out from the crowd and take a chance? All of their achievements would be lost to us. Instead, they chose to give people hope and to fight for change.

What if _you_ took a chance, gave it your all, stood up for something you believed in? There's no telling what you might do!

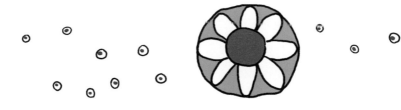

One of the hardest things to do is to speak your **mind** when everyone else thinks differently from you. But if you **speak** up, you may **find** that others agree with you and were afraid to say anything for fear of rejection.

And if you believe something in your **heart** — REALLY **believe** in it — then you can't help but speak your mind anyway... whether anyone present **agrees** with you or not.

Be **true** to your heart
and to your mind
and to your **soul**...
and no matter where you go...
there's no **mountain**
you can't climb.

Being a Girl Who Rocks Can Mean...

Being brave,
being athletic,
being intelligent,
being fabulous,
being super,
being funny.

But mostly it means
being you
and the combination of
traits, talents,
and personal qualities
that make you who
you are!

May you always laugh
and dance and sing.
May your light
light the way
of another.
May you stay true
to the inner flame
that makes your
heart yours.

May all your days be
very special,
very excellent,
very starlike...
for no reason other
than the obvious...

You are a
very special,
very excellent,
very starlike person...
and you deserve that.

Like a Rainbow, you bring
color to ordinary places.

Like a sunset,
you add brilliance.

Like a River,
you know the way.

With the patience of the
forests, you wait for
your dreams to grow.

And like the most special
flower in the garden...

You grow stronger
and more beautiful
every day.

You Totally Rock!

Always Remember that.